MW01204903

Narcissistic Fathers

*Dealing with a Self-Absorbed
Father and Healing from
Narcissistic Abuse*

Copyright © Andrea Hart, 2019

All rights reserved. No part of this publication may be reproduced, stored, or transmitted in any form or by any means, electronic, mechanical, photocopying, recording, scanning, or otherwise without written permission from the publisher. It is illegal to copy this book, post it to a website, or distribute it by any other means without permission.

Designations used by companies to distinguish their products are often claimed as trademarks. All brand names and product names used in this book and on its cover are trade names, service marks, trademarks, and registered trademarks of their respective owners. The publishers and the book are not associated with any product or vendor mentioned in this book. None of the companies referenced within the book have endorsed the book.

First edition

2

Table of Contents

1

Introduction

If you were raised by an emotionally damaged and self-absorbed father, like I was, you may have accumulated a lifetime's worth of abuse, manipulation, and rejection. You might go through life having lingering feelings of anger and resentment towards your father, and the inability to cope with the traumatic experiences prevent you from creating meaningful relationships and friendships.

In this book, you will get a better understanding of the narcissistic personality disorder played out in fatherhood, and how it can destroy your sense of self. You will learn to recognize narcissistic traits and tendencies, so you don't fall prey to your father's lies and manipulation, and I will present to you proven techniques that could help you overcome emotional and psychological trauma.

You are not alone in this journey; this is very important to understand deeply. An important factor for the healing process and to help you live your life fully is to gain awareness and information about narcissism and narcissistic parents. Therefore, I commend you for picking up this book, it is a very good start. It is the start of your path to recovery from narcissistic abuse and emotional trauma. It can help you bring back your sense of self and confidence to overcome adversity. I don't recommend you let it stand alone though. Read as much as you can about the topic and other people's experiences. Perhaps even take it a step further with the methods I suggest or other methods that you find on your way. With realistic techniques and proven methods, you are not powerless to deal with your narcissistic father.

Important disclaimer

Everything in this book is from personal experience and research and does not serve as professional advice within the area of Narcissism and Narcissistic Personality Disorder. Please consult a licensed professional before attempting any techniques outlined in this book.

You should always consult a doctor, a specialist, or a professional therapist before engaging in any treatment. You should also consult with a doctor or a professional therapist if you suspect that you might suffer from a disorder.

No warranties of any kind are expressed or implied. I cannot make any guarantees of results nor guarantee that you will benefit from any of the advice I present in this book.

2

Narcissism

My Father

I always had to make a special effort to please my father when around him. I never felt safe enough to relax and just be myself, and I knew that at any time my father might switch moods if I was not careful. I knew I had to show excessive appreciation for the smallest things he might do for me otherwise he would get upset, disappointed, angry, or some other form of discontent, and I would know it instantly. I learned exactly what I had to do to keep him happy, and what

I had to refrain from doing. I could sense a mile away what mood he was in, and I learned to say and do the exact right things to keep him from yelling or creating a very tense and unpleasant atmosphere. I knew I had to laugh at his jokes to keep him happy, this was very important.

My father often told me that he wished to be just like the Godfather. A powerful man who family and friends would go to for money, so he could hand out amounts to the extent that he felt they deserved his help. He was yearning to be powerful and for people to respect him and probably also fear him a little or a lot.

He always wanted to be taken very seriously and to have his need for attention and acknowledgment met instantly. It was my job to praise him and make sure that I listened when he spoke, or he would be very disappointed. And as you probably know, disappointment is huge for a narcissist. Because I learned to take him that seriously, I thought for many years in my childhood that he was in fact God. I loved him so much and felt oddly very close to him because of his extreme intensity. In my late teenage years, I cried myself to sleep every night because he constantly rejected me. I was about 18 years old when I discovered that he was, in fact, not God. I spent the following years struggling with pain and trying to heal.

A few years back at the age of 32, I stood up to him and chose something different for myself than what he wanted. What I had subconsciously anticipated all my life happened. If I didn't succumb to his rules and wishes and let him have the power, he would cut ties and eliminate me from his life. Of course, I could not risk being tossed out as a kid who loved and needed her father, and hence, I would always be loyal to his commands, but as an adult, I had a choice. It only took one disobedient act, and he decided I was disloyal thus a persona non grata to him. He declared that he didn't want to speak to me again.

Of course, this was very harsh for me, but in all honesty, the real damage had happened many years prior. I sometimes wonder if it was a blessing in disguise because not only has my life been easier since, but my healing has also gone faster than when he was actively a part of my life.

To my knowledge, my father hasn't been diagnosed with narcissism by a professional, but narcissists rarely are. But his level of self-absorbed megalomania has made me want to get to the bottom of narcissism and particularly narcissistic fathers. In my adult life, I have had my share of problems with self-absorbed partners, and in my healing process I wanted to understand what growing up with a narcissistic parent does to a child throughout his or her entire life – not just in childhood.

You will probably relate to a majority of what I present in this book, and there might be some parts you don't relate to at all. This is normal since we all have had our own unique experiences with narcissistic fathers. Every narcissist is different and is never *just* a narcissist, but there are similar traits that are always there as you will learn.

***

What is Narcissistic Personality Disorder and what it isn't?

Narcissism is a word that is used—and sometimes misused—to label a type of mental disorder. In reality, narcissism is not a "dirty" word. Practically all of us have narcissistic traits that can actually be good for us. After all, there's nothing wrong with having a sense of healthy self-regard. It's good for our self-esteem because we know our capabilities and self-worth. However, when love for one's self becomes a deep preoccupation, it becomes a Narcissistic Personality Disorder (NPD).

Based on the definition of the Diagnostic and Statistical Manual of Mental Disorders, NPD is a pervasive pattern of an unrealistic sense of grandiosity, an inflated sense of self-importance, a lack of empathy, and an unhealthy need for admiration.

People with NPD truly believe that they are superior to most anyone they interact with. They have the tendency to associate themselves with people who are unique or possess gifts or traits that could enhance their self-esteem. They feel the need to do this because they have fragile egos underneath their mostly tough exterior.

Because their egos are too delicate, they could not tolerate criticisms, defeat, or rejection. They always seek attention and want other people to think highly of them. If they are criticized, they overreact and go into a rage. And since they cannot lash out at their critics, they turn to people that they can intimidate and torment—family members.

As mentioned, everyone has a socially acceptable level of narcissism. It is a trait that each of us exhibits to a greater or lesser degree. It may be hard to believe but a bit of narcissism is good for us because it allows us to see ourselves through rose-colored glasses. It bolsters our confidence and gives us enough boost to take risks and reach our life goals.

A little bit of narcissism can help in mustering the courage to ask a stranger out on a date or ask for a pay raise from the boss. It makes each person special. It only becomes problematic when the person feels too special.

When a person displays an extreme manifestation of the trait, it is a sign of pathological narcissism. It is so severe that the narcissistic traits impair a person's daily functioning. The dysfunction comes in the form of conflicts in relationships caused by the lack of empathy and intimacy. It may also arise when attention-seeking and grandiosity cause resentment and antagonism.

It must be understood that narcissism falls in a spectrum wherein the disorder sits at the extreme end. To determine where a person's narcissistic tendencies fall in the continuum, the Narcissistic Personality Inventory (NPI) is commonly used. The NPI assesses the level of modesty, assertiveness, the inclination to lead, and willingness to manipulate others. Individuals whose scores fall above the standard deviation are identified as narcissists, while those whose scores fall anywhere along the normal range of the scale are considered to have a fundamentally sound and healthy personality.

When there is a pervasive disturbance in an individual's ability to manage emotions and maintain healthy relationships, there is a clear dysfunction that needs to be addressed.

The Many Faces of Narcissism

To understand narcissism is to realize that narcissism has many faces. There are the stereotypical narcissistic traits that are prevalent in pop culture depictions—*Mad Men's* Don Draper*, Beauty and the Beast's* Gaston, *Gone Girl's* Amy Dunne, *The Devil Wears Prada's* Miranda Priestly and the list goes on. Each one of them presents the most recognizable traits of a narcissist.

While the depictions in movies and television are not wrong, it would be a mistake to assume that all narcissists care about fame, fortune, appearance, vanity, or prestige. Focusing on the stereotypical traits runs the risk of failing to recognize the red flags that have nothing to do with the most recognizable traits.

There are communal variety of narcissists that spend their lives helping others. They are extremely altruistic that they can be considered self-sacrificing martyrs. In this respect, they don't fall into the stereotypical traits, but they are still identified as narcissists.

Contrary to popular belief, highly introverted individuals can also be narcissistic. They are known as vulnerable narcissists who are typically sensitive and temperamental. They don't display grandiosity or superiority, but their egos are just as inflated and as fragile as their extroverted and flamboyant counterparts. Some of them see themselves as misunderstood geniuses and they believe that the world fails to recognize how special they are.

What all types and subtypes of narcissists have in common is their preoccupation with self-enhancement. They are so obsessed with distinguishing themselves from the rest because they truly feel that they are superior to others. Their thoughts, words, and behaviors always lead to a feeling of distinction. If they can separate themselves from others, it makes them feel invincible. The feeling of superiority and distinction soothes them because, in reality, they are struggling to keep it together. After all, they do not have a stable sense of self. This instability makes them unsatisfied with themselves.

When narcissists don't get the attention and the admiration that they crave, they might exhibit both shame and anger. Many of them tend to go on an aggressive outburst that can be violent and scary to those on the receiving end of the backlash. It's their defense mechanism against disappointment and rejection.

Narcissists treat disappointments as breaches to their core and the thick layer of grandiosity is being attacked and weakened. This signifies that narcissists are not oblivious to their problematic traits. They do have insight into their personality, and they acknowledge that other people see them in less than positive light. The difference is that they don't see it as a problem, which indicates how highly they think of themselves.

One theory suggests that narcissistic subtypes have deep-seated insecurity and an incoherent sense of self. So, when they are attacked, they either fight back or fall into a deep depression. The grandiose narcissist almost always fights back, and the vulnerable narcissist gets depleted and depressed. The reaction would always depend on the type of narcissist a person is.

Nature or Nurture: Are Narcissists Made or Born?

Adults may develop a sense of excessive self-regard during their childhood based on their inconsistent experiences with their parents. This is particularly evident when parents refused to acknowledge their achievements or never bragged about their accomplishments and successes. This might have removed that healthy dose of narcissism that could have given the children a boost of confidence in life as they face new challenges growing up.

Narcissistic tendencies can manifest early in life. Preschoolers who displayed aggressive and attention-seeking behavior are more likely to end up as narcissistic adults. However, this does not mean that they are trapped in that narcissistic bubble. Parenting styles, social and cultural environments, and influences of relationships can encourage or deter the development of narcissistic behavior.

Different parenting approaches can have a significant bearing on a child's self-esteem. As we know by now, self-esteem is one of the factors in determining narcissistic tendencies in kids. If kids are brought up in a loving and affectionate environment, where the parents show interest in their kids' activities, the kids will grow up believing they are truly worthy individuals. A healthy dose of self-worth boosts self-esteem high enough but doesn't spill over into narcissism.

On the other hand, parents who overdo things and put their children on a pedestal are unknowingly fostering narcissistic traits. The kids start believing that they deserve to win or that they are better than others when, of course, they are not. It breeds self-entitlement and self-importance.

When there is a pronounced focus on achievement and success, sons and daughters would connect their parents' love and attention to high expectations. This means that if expectations are not met, they are a failure. If children are exposed to this kind of flawed and dangerous thinking, they would always feel that love and attention are only available if they can measure up to unreasonably high standards. This is why everything is a competition for them. They need to be the best in what they do because they feel that the only way to deserve love and attention from their parents is to win at everything. When children enter into adulthood carrying such a burden, they latch onto narcissistic behavior to protect their fragile egos.

Another factor that has a significant influence on a person's development is culture. This is evident in the comparisons between cultures across states and across the globe. Urban cities have higher rates of NPDs compared to rural cities. This is not to say there are no narcissists in remote towns in the countryside; they just don't show up in numbers like they do in competitive cities like New York or Los Angeles.

People who are raised in a more collectivist culture tend to be less self-absorbed. This is because, in their culture, the needs of the group are prioritized over the needs of the individual. They learn this early in life and instilled in their upbringing and carried through to adulthood. This is a far cry from a culture that fosters self-promotion and focuses on individual accolades.

It cannot be denied that childhood experiences play a big role in the development of a person's personality. In the same respect, the combined influences of nature and nurture can influence the narcissistic traits of children, in that, the environment can either strengthen or weaken those traits.

Different Types of Narcissism

Narcissism is so widely used in mainstream culture that it is used indiscriminately to describe behaviors that don't accurately depict what the term represents. It has become an umbrella term used to refer to people who think that the entire world revolves around them. It does not help that reality shows have perpetuated the inaccurate description of a true narcissist.

Although the term "narcissist" is misused and inaccurately depicted, it still has a specific diagnostic definition as stated in the Diagnostic and Statistical Manual of Mental Disorders. The more accurate term to describe people who are extremely self-absorbed and who have an obsession with grandiose fantasies about success, power, and prestige is Narcissistic Personality Disorder.

Not all those who are diagnosed with NPD strictly adhere to the general characterization of narcissism because it exists along a continuum—with healthy self-esteem at one end and extreme NPD at the other end.

There is one main diagnosis, but narcissists can be anywhere in the NPD spectrum. They can be categorized into different types and subtypes based on the personality they exhibit. The three main types are

Classic Narcissists, Vulnerable Narcissists, and Malignant Narcissists.

Classic Narcissists / Grandiose Narcissists

People who fall under this type are also called Grandiose, Exhibitionist, or High Functioning Narcissists. They are essentially the textbook narcissists who seek attention and blow their own horns. Their sense of self-entitlement is extreme because they see themselves as superior to most people they interact with. They think they deserve to be treated as VIPs. They not only crave attention, but they also demand special treatment because they feel that their stature deserves so.

Vulnerable Narcissists

Vulnerable Narcissists are also known as Fragile or Closet Narcissists. They exhibit the same personality traits as the Classic Narcissists, but they do not like to be in the spotlight. They are not the type to seek special treatment although they still feel superior. The distinguishing behavior of vulnerable narcissists is that they use excessive generosity to get the admiration and the attention they to further their sense of self-worth. They would usually put themselves in someone's good graces to win their favor—and that someone is usually in the seat of power or someone important, at the very least.

Malignant Narcissists

Malignant Narcissists are highly toxic because they are extremely manipulative and highly exploitative. They possess so many antisocial traits that they are often identified as sociopaths and psychopaths. They are different from the two other major types because they are known to have a sadistic streak. They enjoy seeing other people suffer because it makes them feel they are above them.

Intending to dominate and control people around them, Malignant Narcissists tend to use aggression to get what they want. They use deceptive tactics to manipulate people into doing things that would shore up their fragile egos. Their complete lack of remorse makes them difficult to deal with.

Researchers and mental health professionals use the major types of narcissists to describe a person with NPD, but they also use sub-types to cover traits that fall in the narcissistic spectrum. These sub-types can be used **together** with the major types to come close to an accurate description if it helps in the diagnosis or behavioral therapy.

Sub-Type 1: Overt vs. Covert

This sub-type describes if the narcissist utilizes methods explicitly or implicitly to get what they need from others. Both sub-types look for the right moment to take advantage of people in pursuit of their selfish goals. Overt narcissists manipulate people openly and make no qualms about it. They can even make their victims feel that it's their fault they were led into the situation they were in.

Covert narcissists are just as arrogant and manipulative as overt narcissists, but they are not vocal about their vanity or their grandiosity. They still harbor overblown fantasies of themselves, but they don't wear their inflated egos out on their sleeves. They are essentially introverted narcissists who downplay their grandiosity but still possess the same toxic personality.

Sub-Type 2: Somatic vs. Cerebral

These sub-types define what narcissists value in themselves or in other people.

Somatic narcissists are those who value their physical appearance so much up to the point where they obsess about their bodies and looks. They spend time in the gym or in front of the mirror not only to appreciate their appearance but also to find flaws that needed to be corrected. They flaunt their toned bodies and brag about their sexual conquests.

Cerebral Narcissists are the classic know-it-alls who try so hard to impress everyone in the room with their intellectual prowess. They go on and on about their accomplishments and they make sure that people know their position in power.

Sub-Type 3: Inverted

Inverted Narcissists are those that attach themselves to other narcissists to feel special. They are only satisfied when they are in relationships with other narcissists. This kind of behavior is believed to have stemmed from childhood abandonment. They latch on to people who have an exaggerated sense of self-worth because they have a need to be loved or looked after. Their traits may seem uncharacteristically narcissistic, but they are described as such because they still fall within the NPD spectrum. The difference is that they are dependent on another narcissist to shore up their need for love, attention, and encouragement.

Can you inherit the traits of a narcissistic parent?

Childhood experiences play a big role in the development of narcissistic personality disorder. There are also types of environments where the risk of developing narcissistic traits is high. Nevertheless, there is a higher chance of vulnerability if the children are genetically predisposed to narcissistic behavior.

Although there is no definitive answer to the question, studies have shown that there is a consistent connection between genetic factors and narcissistic traits. Along with childhood experiences and environmental influences, genetics round up the factors that play a role in the development of narcissistic traits and NPD.

While the effect is not entirely overwhelming, genetic influence is strong enough to have a significant role in the development of the disorder. What this means for you, as a child of a narcissistic father, is that you could have a genetic disposition to acquire the narcissistic traits of your father.

It's not your fault if it something that runs in the family. Also, if your childhood experiences and the environment you were exposed to were largely a negative influence growing up, you are at a greater risk to develop the disorder. But it is also important to keep in mind that a genetic predisposition does not guarantee you'll develop NPD.

3

Your Father, the Narcissist

Kids don't go running around telling everyone that their fathers are narcissists for the simple reason that they have no idea. Children of narcissistic fathers might assume that all fathers are the same. They put their fathers on a pedestal and make them the yardstick against which other men are measured.

But family life is not always smooth sailing. If your father is a narcissist, you'd know about the anger and the rage. After all, you are often at the receiving end of the misplaced fury.

The problem is that, for a young child, the aggression and explosive behavior are difficult to understand. Oftentimes, the child thinks that it's something he or she did that set his father off when the truth is that it doesn't take much to get him triggered. It's not an external trigger but an internal one buoyed by ego and insecurity.

When a father doesn't get his way or gets frustrated, he lashes out at the most vulnerable people around and that's the wife and the children. Kids start to think that they are disappointing their father and they start to feel bad about themselves.

A narcissistic father is likely to demand perfection from his children. Not keeping up with standards or not meeting expectations can easily trigger aggression and rage. As a result, children can feel pressured to excel in school or win in sports competition. They ramp up their talents, improve their grades, and change their appearance just to fulfill their father's wishes. This is sometimes seen but not in all cases.

It is common for a narcissistic father to withhold affection and attention from their children until they satisfy his demands. This is damaging to the kids.

Their needs are being neglected by their own father because they play second fiddle to the needs of the father.

Children of a narcissistic father usually begin to understand when they're already adults and struggling to keep their lives together. At a young age, they do not realize that they have been hurt, abused, and manipulated by their father just to fulfill his needs. Discovering the abuse later in life is a bitter pill to swallow and sometimes the damage done to the psyche is enormous that people have a hard time accepting it and it affects their lives negatively.

Narcissistic fathers have a "tell". They share common behaviors and they conduct themselves in ways that show flashes of narcissism. They are not always obvious, but they exhibit a behavior pattern that leads to the same conclusion—**it is always about them.**

It's not always easy to identify a narcissistic father, but there are telltale signs that they are outright narcissists. When you look back at your childhood, you would learn that:

Dad lacked empathy

Narcissists, in general, don't experience empathy towards other people. They often invalidate the feelings of other people. A narcissistic father, in particular, disregards the feelings of his wife and children, unless they link in some way to his feelings. This lack of empathy breaks down the marriage and the relationship with the children.

Dad used people without them knowing it

A narcissistic father is manipulative and exploitative. He sees his relationship with people as an opportunity to further his ambitions or to achieve success. Since people are charmed by his personality, they are more than willing to cater to his every whim. That's why they don't see themselves as being used as pawns in a narcissist's scheme.

Dad was not always around for the family

A narcissistic father gets plenty of gratification outside the family, so he would rather spend time basking in attention elsewhere rather than deal with the boredom of daily family life. Although he takes pleasure from his family, it does not compare with the satisfaction he gets from other people. The allure of grandiosity is intoxicating to him so he would follow it wherever it leads him, even if it means away from the wife and the children physically and emotionally.

Dad did less parenting

A narcissistic father may find gratification in raising his children simply because he loves them. However, he could only handle so much babysitting and child-rearing. He'd rather get attention than give one. Such is the mindset of a self-absorbed man who craves excitement and longs for activities where the focus is on him and him alone. He'd rather spend his time doing things where he could get pleasure from or where he could boost his already inflated ego. The sad consequence of this is that the mom has to do most of the parenting, which can be draining and exhausting. This can harm the family dynamics if it persists and is not given the attention that it needs.

Dad appreciated his kid when it improves his image

A narcissistic father loves to brag about his children to other people as part of the image he is projecting to everyone. He is so preoccupied with appearances that he is using his kids to add to his appeal and draw more attention to himself. He values smarts, looks, athleticism, and money too much that they become the measure of success and superiority. This puts pressure on the kids to keep up with their father and be the best versions of themselves. This should be okay if the motivation comes from a father's love and validation. However, in a toxic environment when a narcissist lords over the family, the children's main motivations are fear and pressure. This affects the children even through to adulthood because they are already accustomed to an unhealthy and unproductive rewards system that does them no good.

Dad can go on a narcissistic rage when frustrated and upset

A narcissistic father always has a trigger, and it is always something that frustrates or upsets them. Since he has high expectations of his wife and children, anything below expectations is a trigger. For the kids, it could be falling grades, losing games, or not looking good. Any of these reasons could trigger narcissistic rage. When temper flares up, children can get hurt, not just emotionally, but also physically. The narcissistic father does not acknowledge that there is damage being dealt to the children because he sees them as objects. Family members tiptoe around a narcissistic father because they are trying to prevent a rage.

Dad gave sporadic attention to his children

Because it is always about him, he would give attention to his children only when it suits him. Affection and attention are given in spurts if given at all. This can be frustrating to a child who only wants what's normally given unconditionally by a parent. As a result, the child feels he or she does not deserve love and affection and takes the blame for being deficient.

Dad had a wild imagination

Dad exaggerated about most anything, especially when it comes to his achievements. He made them appear more than what they truly were. He had great fantasies of success and prestige and he believed they were real. He had a grandiose outlook on life and that he was the center of the universe. This is why his ambitions and goals are bordered on unrealistic and sometimes eccentric.

Dad didn't like being criticized

Criticisms, constructive or not, always stung dad's fragile ego. Dad didn't take criticism well because it is the one thing that brought him back from fantasy to reality. Instead of taking the criticisms and using them to work on himself, dad would rather cut off the critics out of his life and virtually anyone whom he saw as people who could destroy the fantasy, he had built for himself.

Dad was charismatic

If your dad is charismatic, he can be the life of the party and everyone is drawn to him like a moth to a flame. He exudes a charm that captivates people he interacts with. Although it does not necessarily mean that charisma equates to narcissism, it increases the allure that a person has over others. And when a man has great allure, he can use it to get people to do his bidding. It paves the way for manipulation to take place.

He could make you feel that you were the center of his world, but only because it was part of the image he was trying to project to everyone. He can just as easily drop you and move on like you never mattered at all, especially when he already got what he wanted out of the act. You never really got his full attention because his mind is elsewhere.

Levels of Narcissism

Many of the narcissistic traits discussed above are probably spot on and some may not have manifested at all. Fathers who exhibit narcissistic traits don't always go on extreme behavior when they feel threatened in some way. Some of them show subtle hints of narcissism that could easily turn full-blown with the slightest provocation. It all depends on the situation and the level of narcissism.

Psychologists have long been interested in measuring the level of narcissism to help in the diagnosis of the disorder. They have devised a wide variety of methods to assess where in the narcissistic disorder spectrum an individual falls in.

The most common method of assessing narcissism is the use of standardized self-report measures, which contain multiple items that are measured in subscales which can make a fine distinction between degrees of narcissistic traits. Of course, you can only measure your father's level of narcissism if he agrees to such an assessment, the likelihood of which is slim to nil.

You cannot get an accurate measure of the degree of narcissism, but you can determine if you are being raised by a narcissistic parent. If your father exhibits all of the narcissistic traits discussed above, then you can place him on the extreme end of the disorder spectrum.

4

Effects of Narcissistic Parenting

Narcissistic fathers will always find a way to make everything about them. They will steal their kids' thunder and eclipse their feelings because their profound need for praise and attention subverts the needs of their children. Because of their frail egos, there are overly sensitive to criticisms and censures.

Children are aware of their father's sensitivities and they know that it only takes little provocation to anger them. So, they learn (perhaps the hard way) to tiptoe around their father's emotional minefield just to avoid triggering anger or the withdrawal of affection and attention.

What's fascinating is that children of a narcissistic father can be very perceptive that they pick up on their father's emotional vulnerability. At a young age, they have the cognitive ability to adjust to the situation by complimenting their father or meeting or exceeding his expectations. In a way, the children are taking care of their father in the hope that he would get back to taking care of his kids. The danger here is that the children run the risk of losing touch with their own needs and emotions in exchange for their father's affection. The reality is that there is no guarantee that their father will change and return the love and attention that they sorely crave for.

Effect on Young Children

Children of a narcissistic father tend to lose their own identity because they are focused on making their father happy that they become what their father wants them to be instead of being what they truly are. They grow up not trusting their instincts because they always doubt their decisions. As long as their father's presence looms large in their life, they would question their judgment in all matters.

Narcissism takes a toll on the children's emotional and mental well-being. They have difficulty expressing their feelings because they fear that asserting themselves can lead to rejection. The traumatic experiences they had as a child would continue to linger through to adulthood. They lose their sense of self and this presents a lot of issues in their lives as they enter into relationships and have a family of their own.

Effect on Teenage Kids

Teenagers will find that their narcissistic father is unpredictable and explosive. They have a hard time understanding the situation they are in. The enormous pressure to fit into a personality mold set out for them creates an internal conflict. They are forced to push aside their personalities to comply with what their narcissistic father requires them to do. Since they are still trying to find their own identities, they are often confused about their situation. When they fall short of expectations, they are verbally abused, grounded, or avoided.

Because teenagers cannot make sense of the manipulation and abuse, they begin to internalize feelings of deep shame which eventually turns into self-loathing for not being able to fully comply with their narcissistic fathers' wishes. They begin to think that they are lacking. Until they meet the high expectations set out for them, they are made to feel that they are not deserving of love and attention. They grow up with absent self-identity and gravitate towards people similar in trait to their fathers because they couldn't handle being loved the way they ought to be.

The need to be loved and the innate need for attention that every teenager has are needs that are not fully met by the narcissistic father. Teenagers are becoming more of a challenge for him than the younger children because they are developing a more critical and independent mind and can be a handful as teenagers often are. The father might not find it as amusing and stimulating to be around teenagers, and he will reject them. For this reason, kids might feel the pain from the neglect increase in the teen years.

Effect on Adult Children

Daughters of Narcissistic Fathers

Daughters of narcissistic fathers often feel that they had to compete with their siblings for their father's love, time, and attention. They harbor the feeling that their needs are not met. While they get the occasional compliments from Dad, the criticisms are the ones that linger in their minds—the insensitive comments on weight, appearance, failings, and his disappointment when they fail to please him. This becomes a concern because daughters tend to carry the negative perception about themselves into adulthood. Even if they find success in their careers and relationships, they will always doubt their capabilities and self-worth. It adds to the long list of obstacles that they need to hurdle just by being a female.

In terms of relationships, daughters raised by a narcissistic father often carry the fear of being dumped for someone more beautiful, more fit, or more successful and they often feel the urge to overperform to be loved and wanted. This is because they feel that they are never enough for someone or they are always lacking in something. As a result, they might want to avoid commitment altogether. They protect their heart when in a relationship, but they take on a narcissistic role as a defense mechanism. Either way, daughters set themselves up to lose.

Without a father's love, attention, and adoration, daughters will always want validation of their specialness. With this validation, daughters of narcissistic fathers will always feel that they don't deserve love.

As an adult, daughters of narcissistic fathers realize the harsh truths and negative effects of a toxic relationship plagued by unrealistic expectations, lack of attention, and manipulative actions. The realizations usually don't just come out of the blue; they often have to be pushed out of the recesses of the mind through therapy.

Just like other daughters of narcissistic fathers, you might also discover later in life that:

- You develop low self-esteem because you are made to believe that you are not enough.

- You equate your value as a person based on what you do and accomplish. If you are winning at something, you think highly of yourself, but if you are failing, you consider yourself worthless. This stemmed from the attention you get from your narcissistic father when you are succeeding for instance in school and the abuse you receive when you are not living up to his expectations. As an adult, a time you might feel better is when you take harmful substances that you have difficulty quitting. The next thing you know, you're already hooked on "feel-good" drugs.

- You are never genuinely praised because you never meet the unrealistic expectations of your father. Whatever praise you get, it is part of keeping up with appearances to maintain the grandiose image that your father created. You realize that you are criticized more than you are praised.

- You are in a co-dependence relationship because your narcissistic father manipulated you into thinking that you can't live without him. It is a way to maintain control over you. There was never a real father-daughter relationship to begin with. Even the thought of leaving instills an enormous feeling of guilt, which bolsters the idea that you really cannot function well without your father.

- You feel the need to beat everyone because you are raised in an environment that fosters competition. You and your siblings compete for the little attention that your father sporadically gives. You equate worthiness with being the best. This not only puts pressure on yourself, but it also strains the relationships you have with everyone else.

- You lose your true identity because you are forced to be someone you're not just to please a man who sets you up to fail in life. You deny your feelings and emotions because you are expected to feel a certain way. As a result, when you are cut loose from the abusive relationship, you realize you do not have goals and desires that are truly your own. This is a scary situation to be in because your thoughts and feelings depend on someone else's bidding.

Sons of Narcissistic Fathers

With fathers who are so competitive and think highly of themselves, sons of narcissistic fathers feel that they can never measure up. This is a tough struggle because narcissistic fathers compete with their own sons in many respects. The problem is that the bar is set so high, it's unrealistic—except for Dad whose grandiosity makes him think that he could achieve the unachievable.

Sons also crave attention from Dad, but they only get it when they meet or exceed expectations. When they fall short, they become at the receiving end of anger and rage. As a result, they are driven to succeed to please the one person that does not really care much about them. They are resigned to the fact that they can't beat their fathers at their own game.

Some sons of narcissistic fathers live life feeling depleted and insecure because they never felt the love and attention that they sought while growing up. Others learn to manipulate and use other people to get attention, thereby morphing into narcissists themselves.

Just like other sons of narcissistic fathers, you might also discover later in life that:

- Your dad competes with you because he knows you are less capable than him. You are an automatic target for his ruthless bullying because you are accessible and powerless to fight back.

- Your dad inflates his achievements to disparage your accomplishments. Nothing is good enough for him even if you become successful in your chosen field. This leaves you feeling deflated and insecure.

- Your father's words become your gospel truths. His rules were strictly enforced that they instilled fear in you. You develop an unhealthy fear of authority figures.

- Your life is controlled by your father that even your dreams and aspirations are not your own. Whatever you are aiming for is most likely what your father told you to aim for. As a result, when you detach from your narcissistic father, you don't know what to do with yourself.

- Your dad may provide for you on a material level, but he is emotionally unavailable. He has no interest in your activities because he considers them a burden and a waste of time. He also thinks that giving you support is you stealing the limelight from him.

- You endure years of emotional abuse that you grow up to be cautious and guarded. You hide your true feelings and emotional needs, which leads to intimacy problems when you enter into a serious relationship.

- You are motivated to succeed only because you want the validation and approval of your father. This makes your success feel hollow and empty.

Long-lasting Effects of Narcissistic Parenting by a Father

When sons and daughters live in the shadow of a narcissistic father, there are long-term effects that may be difficult to reverse. Children who are constantly exposed to paternal narcissism develop a personality influenced by their relationships. Their character and temperament are shaped by the effects of relationships, and they are wired into the biological blueprint, thereby creating a personality that is a mix of genetics and environment.

What happens to the development of personality when children live under the shadow of a narcissistic father? The following effects commonly manifest and linger in adulthood.

1. Lingering self-blame

Emotionally sensitive children long for love and attention from their parents, but if one or both parents are emotionally tone-deaf, children start to believe that they are the problem. They often sacrifice their self-esteem in exchange for the hope that they would be given the attention that they seek. They think that they needed fixing in order to deserve attention. They blame themselves for what is missing in their lives even if it is evident that their narcissistic father explicitly withholds what their kids need.

2. Avoidant attachment

The neglect, abuse, and manipulation of a narcissistic father can make the children question their degree of comfort in their relationships with other people. They may develop avoidant attachment wherein they shut people out as a fear management mechanism. They fear that the people they depend on will hurt and leave them. So, instead of taking the risk, they just avoid getting too attached to them.

3. Anxious attachment

This is the opposite of avoidant attachment. It is a form of insecure attachment wherein people chase after love and attention with loved ones. At times, they angrily pursue the connection they crave from people they love. They always question why they are not getting the attention that they seek. This creates relationship issues later in life because it can be suffocating to people who are being pursued.

4. Neediness

A narcissistic father can instill fear in their children by using scare tactics. One of these tactics is threatening them that their needs will not be provided. They do so by becoming compulsive caretakers, so the children depend on them for the things they need. When children do not receive these needs, they panic and seek reassurance from friends or loved ones. Their fears can only be alleviated when their needs are immediately met. As a result, they become clingy to their partners because they are terrified when their needs are not fulfilled.

5. Extreme independence

Children of a narcissistic father may abandon emotional intimacy because they believe that people cannot be trusted. They become fiercely independent individuals who avoid unreliable people. This is not sustainable in the long term because everyone needs someone to rely on and to have a nurturing relationship with. Those who avoid intimacy could trigger the neediness in them which leads back to anxious attachment.

Conversely, children who have sensitive temperaments are more likely to do the opposite and become compulsive caretakers. They see it as living and enjoying the emotional and physical nurturance vicariously through the people they take care of.

6. Parentification of children

Sensitive children of a narcissistic father can become parentified, which is a role reversal wherein a child takes the role of a parent to fill in the emotional void created by a parent in the first place. This makes young kids extremely mature for their age because they organize their lives around the happiness of their parents and of others in adulthood. They do so to boost the self-esteem of their narcissistic father to prevent rage and anger. They cater to their father's every whim. Parentified children can grow up hating their own needs and wants, thinking they are a burden to their loved ones.

7. Becoming narcissists

Children with a stubborn streak and aggressive temperament are likely to respond to paternal narcissism by mimicking their father's narcissistic traits. It is a classic case of "if you can't beat them, join them". They strive to be the smartest, loudest, or prettiest because they want to feel important. These children are likely to end up narcissistic in adulthood.

8. Foreshortened sense of future

An extremely abusive narcissistic father can traumatize their children. When they are constantly terrified of their father, they are likely to take a fearful approach in life. They are always reminded of the abuse that can cause chronic anxiety, depression, and a negative outlook of the future. They become overly fixated on surviving in the present that they have a foreshortened sense of future. When living in the present becomes a constant threat, it is almost impossible to think of the future. They lose the ability to enjoy life and mapping out their life for the future does not give them something to look forward to.

Is there an upside to a narcissistic father?

Believe it or not, there are some potential benefits to narcissistic parenting. The keyword here is *potential* because it is up to the parent to turn the narcissism into something positive.

Take the case of the narcissistic father who invests in himself because he wants people to see him as the brilliant person that he created in his mind. Since he considers his child as an extension of himself, he also wants his child to keep up. He celebrates good results or victories in the individual competition so that the child feels appreciated. More than that, the crowd would see both father and child in a favorable light. In this sense, the child is getting something out of the toxic relationship and not just a lifetime of criticisms.

The narcissistic father becomes a fierce advocate of his child if he stands to benefit from it. If people see him as the "father of the year" kind of guy by spending more time with his child, then he would keep spending time with the kid. This is beneficial to the child because they at least share positive and nurturing experiences. It may appear to be a shallow benefit, but it is a huge thing to get out of a narcissistic father who normally does not appreciate sharing the limelight with a child nor a partner.

5

The Enabling Mother

The Enabling Parent

In a family where the narcissistic father dominates, the role of the mother is overshadowed. The mother often takes a backseat and lets the father rule the family with an iron fist. This is highly unnatural and symptomatic of dysfunction that is tolerated and allowed to persist to the detriment of the family in general and the scapegoat child in particular.

In a narcissistic home, there is a golden child and a scapegoat child. The narcissistic father picks these roles in the family and it stays that way until some circumstances flip the roles around. The golden child is the conformer who is constantly pressured to measure up. He or she loses their sense of self to play the part that the narcissistic father choses for him. The upside is that he or she gets all the love, nurturing, and attention. The love-bombing creates a cognitive dissonance because the golden child is exposed to pressure which he or she struggles with but wouldn't want to give up the love and attention.

On the other hand, the scapegoat is always at the receiving end of criticisms, shaming, and abuse. He or she is blamed for their weaknesses and shortcomings even though he or she was put in a position to fail.

The presence of the golden child and the scapegoat child in a narcissistic home drives a wedge between members of the family. It promotes conflicts because the children turn on each other and compete for their father's attention. The narcissistic father sets this up so he can get his narcissistic supply or sustenance to boost his self-esteem.

You know this situation all too well because you might have played one of the roles. But through all the narcissistic maneuvering, where does your mother fit in the dynamics? And the more important question is why didn't she intervene the way a mother is expected to do? The answer is not easy, but you knew all along that your mother had failed you for allowing the abuse to persist for a very long time.

What this tells us is that your mother is an enabler. Narcissism is no different from addiction because your father is addicted to attention and control. He is not willing to relinquish the power that he has over the members of the family; not even share the power with his wife. As a result, the mother is relegated to be an observer with no real say in family matters.

In situations where the mother subscribes to the idea that the needs of the narcissistic father are more important than the needs of the children, then the dysfunction is much worse than when a mother chooses to be the passive parent.

The harsh reality is that the enabling mother is a second abuser regardless if she is the kinder parent or the equally horrible parent. Each time she lets a narcissistic abuse slide, she is contributing to the suffering of the children, especially the scapegoat.

More often than not, the enabling mother sides with the narcissistic father and perpetuates the scapegoating of a child for all the wrong things happening in the family. The more she throws support to the father, the more she encourages the abuse and manipulation.

Dissonance

Sometimes, it creates confusion for the child (especially the teenager and the adult child) because the enabling mother is the kinder parent who is innately nurturing and loving. However, when her actions don't match the child's view of her, it creates cognitive and emotional dissonance. The one person who could help the child is nothing but a weak side-kick to the main abuser.

What's more jarring is that even in her passive actions, she is allowing the narcissistic behavior to thrive. The child, especially the scapegoat, struggles to understand the behavior but remains confused, which adds a burden to his already hard life.

Self-Preservation

No matter how real it can get, the enabling mother is not going to see the situation the way a scapegoat child would. She is not cognizant of the fact that even if she is empathetic to the emotionally tormented child, her downplaying the narcissistic abuse damages her relationship with her child.

The enabling mother is extremely loyal to the narcissistic father up to the point that she apologizes for his abuses. She is doing this because of self-preservation. It must not be forgotten that she, too, is a victim of the narcissist. She is so manipulated and brainwashed that she, herself, has lost her voice and true identity. She has already suffered the same abuse that her child is currently suffering. Her silence and inaction are her way to shut down and keep her sanity intact.

Why enablers stay?

An enabling mother chooses to stay in a toxic home with the narcissistic father for a variety of reasons. It could be because of religious beliefs about marriage and divorce. It could be due to financial reasons or unwillingness to give up the comfortable life. It could also be because she is acting out an intergenerational pattern of narcissistic-enabler dynamics. Among the reasons, perhaps the one that carries the most weight is fear—fear of the repercussions of leaving. She fears that her narcissistic husband would make things even more difficult for her and the children. She doesn't have the confidence and the strength to fight a narcissist especially when it comes to dealing with divorce.

The Role of the Mother

In a narcissistic home, the mother has to be the balancing force in the family. An enabling mother is not capable of finding the very delicate balance because she has already sided with the abuser from the get-go. The moment an enabling mother ignores the needs of the children, it tips the balance in favor of the narcissistic father.

- In the midst of abuse and manipulation, the mother has to intercede and meet the children on their emotional level and validate their feelings. This action helps them feel they are understood. There is no judgment in what they had failed to do, especially when the expectations are unreasonably high.

- The mother must send a message to her children that their feelings make sense and they have every right to feel the way they do when being punished or scapegoated by a narcissistic father.

- The mother has to acknowledge that there is a problem. Children of a narcissistic father feel that their struggles are being dismissed or minimized when their mother refuses to recognize that the problem is real and not some fantasy.

- The mother has to explain to the children that the bad situation they are in is not their fault. The blame that their narcissistic father placed upon them is unfair and unfounded. This lifts the heavy burden on their shoulders.

- The mother has to tell the truth. A narcissistic father thrives on lies and trickery, which are the hallmarks of manipulation and exploitation. Telling the truth about their father's extreme reactions can help them realize that the anger and rage coming from him is not their fault nor their responsibility. This part is a delicate matter to handle because children have different levels of maturity when it comes to handling the truth. By exercising best judgment, the truth can be told responsibly without a hint of anger or resentment towards the father.

- The mother must not demonize the narcissistic father to the children. It is almost impossible to temper feelings towards a highly abusive spouse, but the mother must resist the desire to put the father in a bad light around the children. The mother can talk more openly about the personality disorder when the children get older.

- A mother must fill the gaps that the narcissistic father is unable to fill. This means giving unconditional love, encouraging good work, supporting reasonable competence, empathizing, and reinforcing confidence. When the children feel that they are getting the love and support they need, they can develop resilience and toughness to recover from difficulties and challenges.

6

Emotionally Healthy Parents

There is a growing number of children and adolescents diagnosed with various mental health disorders. Unfortunately, not all of these children receive the professional treatment they need to improve their situations. The main reason is the shortage of pediatric mental health care providers.

Although treatment is crucial in managing health issues among children, it is just important to help parents raise emotionally healthy children. It is bad enough that parents cannot identify the problem before it gets worse, but it's extremely worrying that many parents are emotionally unhealthy, to begin with. If they cannot deal with their own emotional demons, how can they expect to manage their children's emotional struggles?

Emotionally healthy parents are more likely to raise emotionally healthy children. Conversely, narcissistic parents are more likely to raise children with narcissistic tendencies.

With so much attention given to the topic of narcissistic parents, the negative side of parenting is unnecessarily magnified. It is important to know the difference between emotionally healthy parents and emotionally unhealthy parents. It is fair to assume that narcissistic parents are emotionally unhealthy that is why the children they raise struggle in life as adults.

Emotionally healthy parents possess many of the following traits and abilities.

- They notice when their child is struggling.

  At the first sign of a behavioral change in their child, emotionally sound parents would not dismiss it as just a phase that their child would eventually grow out of. Parents recognize that small behavioral patterns can lead to problematic behaviors later in life if they are not addressed. Temper tantrums, exaggerated focus on video games, and aggressive behavior in school are some of the issues that can manifest in small doses early in life that could become full-blown problems in the future.

- They are sensitive and in tune with their children's needs.

When something is bothering a child, he or she may not be able to convey it properly in words, so they communicate in other ways by throwing a tantrum or exhibiting aggressive behavior to get some attention. Parents who are in tune with the needs of their child would encourage open communication so they could get to the bottom of the problem and involve the child in finding a solution.

- They are not reactive and not defensive.

Parents who react defensively can cause their children to shut down. This makes finding out their true problems and struggles very difficult. Emotionally healthy parents would work to gain their child's trust so that he or she becomes comfortable enough to talk and communicate honestly.

- They spend quality time with their children.

  Spending quality time means parents offer uninterrupted attention to the children to drive home a point—the kids are their number one priority. It is an opportunity to share an activity that they all can enjoy. It also gives the parents a chance to interact and communicate with the children when their defenses are down. It creates an environment where trust and honesty organically occur.

- They don't force children to open up to them.

  Many parents approach their children authoritatively that they come across as villains out to ruin their children's life. When children refuse to open up about their struggles, forcing them to do so would not make them talk. This is especially true among teenagers. Emotionally healthy parents would not force the issue; instead, they would find someone who knows how to talk to their child. It could be an aunt, a grandmother, a teacher, or someone the kids trust. Letting the kids know that they can talk to someone aside from their parents will encourage them to open up and ease the burden. This is particularly helpful when the kids' struggles involve the parents themselves.

- They give children the emotional support they need at the first sign of real trouble.

There is no shame in getting help especially when children are going through something. When children exhibit anger, anxiety, fear, and other unusual signs, emotionally healthy parents will get them the proper help that they need. They would consult mental health professionals, teachers, or counselors. They recognize that their children's mental and emotional well-being outweigh how they are viewed as parents. Their children's welfare takes precedence over what others think of them.

- They take care of their own emotional health and overall well-being.

Although the children's needs come first, it is equally important to keep the parent's emotional health in check. Truth be told, children are instinctive, and they are naturally in tune with their parent's moods. Emotionally healthy parents recognize that they cannot fully mask what they are feeling. That's why parents need to be in good mental and emotional shape so that they can relate at a deeper level with their kids.

- They express emotions appropriately.

   Parents tend to be reactive when their children did something wrong. It is a form of defense mechanism because they know that bad behavior would be seen as a reflection of their parenting style. Emotionally healthy parents react sensitively so that they don't discourage their children from opening up about their struggles.

- They can control their behavior when faced with challenges.

   Challenges can come in spades and can overwhelm even the most stable person. Parents who are emotionally well-grounded don't break under pressure. This is because they keep problems and challenges in perspective. They have the sense to change the circumstance of their lives especially situations that are causing them stress.

- They know how to be happy and enjoy life because they have a support system they can turn to in times of emotional difficulties.

Emotionally healthy parents can influence and nurture their children's ability to lead emotionally healthy lives. These parents succeed because they recognize problems and find ways to solve them before the damage becomes irreparable.

7

Understanding and Relating to a Narcissistic Father

Who is the adult child of a narcissistic father?

Not all children of narcissists are the same, but they sure share common traits. The degree to which they manifest issues and problems depends on the severity of the father's narcissism. It hits the child hard especially when there are no supportive influences in the child's life. The frequent presence of grandparents, teachers, or adult relatives during childhood could cushion the blow of the father's narcissism. Unfortunately, a support system is not always available for a child that's why the narcissistic abuse thrived.

A narcissistic home is especially destructive when a narcissistic father only has a few close friends who are equally insensitive to the feelings and needs of the child. In this kind of environment, the narcissistic father sets the rules and creates an atmosphere of terror where the child feels there is little to no chance of escape.

The narcissistic father instills the view that his child is not an independent being. The irony of this is that he wants his child to depend on him but he has no interest in proper child-rearing. He refuses to tend to the needs of the child and is only interested in pleasing himself. He cannot relate to the child's needs because he is too focused on his own needs.

The adult child of a narcissistic father is not given the opportunity to be a separate being. There is an osmotic relationship created by the father wherein he refuses to recognize the psychological and emotional boundaries between himself and his child.

The child can be happy if the father is happy and the child must be miserable if the father is miserable. The child is "not allowed" to be happy when the father is miserable because it is perceived as a sign of disloyalty. But it is all right if the situation is reversed.

Early in life, the child is never seen for what he or she truly is. The narcissistic father has attributed characteristics to the child so there is no sense of identity. The problem here is that all the inefficiencies and shortcomings attributed to the father are transferred onto the child. This makes the child feel that he or she is severely defective and unlovable.

There is a strong pressure for the father to conform to the high expectations that he himself created. Being included in the narcissistic umbrella where grandiosity and self-importance flourish, the child is pressured to conform as well. Failing to do so means the child is in for harsh punishment, or worse, be pushed out. Since the expectations are unreasonable, the child usually fails. The more frequently failure happens, the more the child feels a complete failure and not deserving of love. This creates an unhealthy view of one's self. On the off chance that the child succeeds, he or she feels it is not a real success because the true self is already identified and linked with failure.

It is common for a child to feel that the right to exist as a separate autonomous being is incomprehensible for the narcissistic father. The sense of self has been twisted and shaped into something resembling that of the father. In that sense, there is no real independence for the child and any attempt to come out of the shell is viewed as a betrayal. The child would then stop finding the true self because doing is greeted with resentment and anger.

As the child matures, he or she learns to distrust the reality of his or her thoughts. As a result, other people are permitted to think for the child. This creates an inner conflict in the child which damages his or her self-worth.

The constant barrage of critical comments and harsh criticisms can make a child paranoid. He or she becomes overly sensitive to remarks that are perceived as attacks. To the child, there is an unfounded belief that everyone is out to hurt him or her deliberately.

When a child accepts the opinions of the narcissistic father as gospel truths, the child does the same to other people who speak with power and authority. This makes a child vulnerable to manipulation and exploitation.

A child who is exposed to a toxic home will find him-/herself being friends with narcissists. This is because he or she has become accustomed to the dynamics of a narcissistic relationship that it is easy to transition. He or she just assumes his or her familiar role but this time, he or she bows down to narcissistic friends. He or she would soon realize that this kind of friendship is not only frustrating but also unfulfilling, just like his or her relationship with his father. What's jarring is that even if he or she recognizes this and is unhappy with the friendship, he or she still tries to win the narcissistic friends' love and approval.

Since a child of a narcissistic father has little love for him-/herself, he or she tries to find love by getting attention even if it means exhibiting objectionable behaviors that put people off.

He or she may deliberately annoy everyone around him or her with an unkempt appearance or poor hygiene. He or she may commit offenses to provoke others as a way to preserve the real self. He or she hopes that they would be embraced and accepted when reverting to the true self. To the child, negative attention is better than no attention at all.

Assailed by critical evaluations and negative labels, the child has no sense of his or her true identity. He or she does not know who he or she is and just assumes the character traits that other people assign to him or her. He or she has no freedom to experiment to find out for him-/herself and he or she ends up feeling that he is no good.

One tragic irony from the whole toxic relationship dynamics is that the adult child may have acquired the many classic narcissistic traits of the father. These narcissistic features include self-centeredness, the desire to be perfect, the need to be right all the time, the inability to take criticisms, the exaggerated need for attention, and the constant need for reassurance that he or she is adored and loved.

The adult child has thus internalized the narcissistic father and may transition from a victim to an abuser. He or she may victimize his or her spouse, children, or friends because he or she has assumed the role of the narcissist parent becoming the monster that he or she despises.

If the adult child desires to achieve autonomy and regain the sense of self, he or she must find ways to cope and protect him-/herself from becoming a full-blown narcissist him-/herself.

Coping and Protecting Yourself

If you are an adult child of a narcissistic father, you might have started to realize just now how toxic the environment was while you were growing up. You are probably learning that you have absorbed all the negative opinions about you even though they are not true. You accepted the wrong opinions as valid and true because you felt guilty about rejecting your father's false view of yourself. He made you believe that you fit the negative profile he fabricated to make you feel insignificant and worthless.

It has taken years to come to the realization, but you may feel a little bit triumphant for the opportunity to get your life back. Hopefully by now, you are realizing that you have to start seeing yourself as you are and not the picture that your narcissistic father painted you to be. You acknowledge that change needs to happen if you want to reverse years of emotional neglect and abuse.

Change will not come easy because your narcissistic father will not change his ways just because you are now wiser about the relationship. If you want to be treated differently, the change must start in how you present yourself with him whenever you get the chance to interact.

You know how narcissism can make you feel, so even if you and your father have not seen each other for long stretches of time, you can recognize it the moment he opens his mouth to give you a negative aesthetic evaluation of yourself as a form of greeting.

A narcissistic father will always find something to attack you with, no matter what you say. He has enough ammunition to cast judgment on you to make you feel stupid, weak, useless, or something else. It has been his approach for the longest time, so there's no way he's going to change knowing full well that his tactics have been effective in demolishing your self-esteem, or whatever's left of it.

It is difficult to respond properly to a demeaning comment if you are oversensitive to critical comments. The way your father makes you feel depends on how sensitive you are to hurtful words. Even if you respond defensively and change the topic of conversation to your strength, the offensive comments thrown at you will always hurt.

Working on your hypersensitivity is one way to prepare yourself to deal with your narcissistic father. Judgment will always be present, but if you learn to acknowledge that everyone has shortcomings, you wouldn't think of yourself as a worthless human being that your father makes you out to be.

The problem with children of narcissistic parents is that they automatically gravitate toward the negative. It is a learned behavior caused by long years of emotional abuse. The negative comments about appearance and performance, even if they are not accurate, stay with the children and gnaw at them. The feelings of unworthiness and unlovability deepen when there is nothing to contradict the parent's false image about their children.

In a toxic relationship, such as the one you have with your father, the affirmation of your positive traits and abilities are probably hard to find. You just don't measure up to the unreasonably high expectations of a delusional and self-absorbed father. What you probably for a long time failed to realize (as children of narcissistic fathers do) is that a father does not fit the image of Superman. For so long, you believed in the perfection of your father because that is the image that he projected to you and to everyone else. The same perfection makes it difficult to find errors and limitations, which only fortifies the notion that your father is, indeed, perfect.

Learning to think that your father is not infallible can make negative words less hurtful. They don't sink so deep and they make you feel less affected. The less affected you are, the more you can focus on finding ways to respond properly.

As an adult child of a narcissistic father, you grow older and try to make a life for yourself without the parental pressures and definitely without the manipulations. However, even as you grow older, you still fall prey to your father's manipulations. You still do what he expects you to do even though you can choose not to do so. But there will come a point where you're no longer willing to tolerate the manipulation.

Living with narcissism is like training to feel inadequate. You learn to hate yourself because your father's demeaning remarks constantly reminded you about your flaws. Even though you know that having flaws is normal, you still feel bad because the way your father treats you magnified your flaws unnecessarily.

How to react to negative comments and criticisms

1. Do not submit to criticisms. No matter how hurt and defeated you feel when your father spews unacceptable comments, you must not defer to the unfounded opinions. Your father will most likely demand that you agree with him immediately, but it doesn't have to be the case. Do not be bullied into an agreement just because your father can't deal with his own

insecurity. Treat the criticisms as opinions and suggestions that you will consider in your own time and when you are in the right frame of mind to evaluate them.

2. Respect your response. You can agree or disagree with what is said about you, but once you respond, let your comments rest. There's no need to explain or act defensively. The more you engage with combatant words, the more you are encouraging the destructive comments.

3. Be firm and noncombative. If a critical remark makes you worry because there might be some truth to it, seek evaluation from people who can help you make changes in yourself. Don't allow your father to make you feel even more inadequate. He is not the best person to criticize you because his criticisms are meant to destroy you and not make you better.

4. Ignore compulsive criticisms. A narcissistic father is a compulsive critic. His criticisms are bolstered by your attention and response. If you argue, deny, or oppose his criticisms, you are showing him that his remarks affect you and it gives him the ammunition to keep attacking until you surrender. If you ignore the destructive criticisms, your father has nothing

to latch on to and the pattern of abuse is disrupted.

5. Use humor to put a narcissist in a vulnerable position. Finding your narcissistic father's weak spot and using humor to embarrass him or put him in a position where he can be self-humiliated by his remarks can stop him cold. If he is embarrassed in the presence of his audience that looks up to him, he would not engage in further discussion about his criticisms about you because your "failures" reflect back on him. And since his image is everything, he would not dare let it be tarnished.

The above suggestions are not going to be easy to carry out. Perhaps you have already experimented with other or similar methods and found just how hard it can be to change behavior towards your father and yourself. You will probably fail over and over again and that's okay. The most important person in your life is you, and if there is one thing, I would love for you to take away from this book, it is to be as good to yourself as you possibly can. This includes quitting self-criticism altogether. Please don't let this be empty words. I mean it. And you are not alone.

Breaking the Codependency Relationship

A father's narcissism revolves around codependency. A narcissistic father demands that his codependent child gets satisfaction when he takes pleasure in his inflated self-image. If the child is constantly criticized while the father relishes his greatness, the stark contrast is magnified. This means that the father relies heavily on his child's misery to lift himself. The child, on the other hand, feels guilt when he or she withholds attention.

The truth is that narcissistic fathers are needy. Their need for attention is dependent on how they can manipulate their children into believing their lies and their rationalizations.

If you find yourself stuck in a codependent situation, you need to try to break free from the clutches of this unfair behavioral pattern. You must understand what is fair to you and to your father by developing your own judgment on who needs and deserves your care.

A narcissistic father's philosophy is that his child cannot say no to him. But as an adult child of a narcissistic father, you can say no, even though the pressure to say otherwise seems too much to bear. The guilt is what's making you surrender to the pressure.

You have to remember that it is not your responsibility to maintain your father's admirable image. You don't have to sacrifice yourself to save your father's reputation, and you will be fine even if he is not.

How then can you develop your own judgment and have the strength to say no even if it greatly disappoints your father? You can do this by observing how non-narcissistic people relate and respond to each other. You have spent much of your life in an unhealthy bubble that you have no clear understanding of how people from the other side carry on with normal relationships. Of course, it does not mean that you can magically escape narcissism's grip just by observing other people. What is being suggested is that the isolation made you blind to what is fair and what is not fair when it comes to the parent-child relationship.

Also, you probably have to accept that your relationship with your father will never be a so-called normal parent-child relationship. He will always be different and toxic, and you need to adjust and protect yourself.

Channeling Anger

Children develop anger for their narcissistic father as they grow up and gradually come to the realization that they had been manipulated as children and are still being manipulated as adults. Anger is not entirely bad if it puts you on the road to recovery and change. However, you may have been raised to conceal anger because you were instructed that negative emotions should never be unleashed by you. That's why there's pent up anger that's just waiting to explode. When it builds up, it takes little provocation to release it.

A narcissistic father sets unrealistic expectations so that he has a reason to be disappointed when you don't measure up. This gives him a feeling of superiority and the more he does it, the more he is convinced that he is above you. This is enough to fuel your anger. What you have to realize is that by showing anger, you are giving your father more ammunition. To him, your anger is a validation that he is right about the negative things he says about you. The more you succumb to expressing anger, the more he wrests control over you.

Your anger should of course not reside inside you either, and a healthy outlet such as therapy is recommendable.

Future Relationship with Your Father

Your father's controlling words and gestures will never change. The level of impact may tone down a little bit, but it does not make it less hurtful. As you grow older, you should review your understanding of narcissism as you are doing right now. The more you understand what it is, the more you will find yourself starting to disregard the narcissistic behavior. It will not be immediate. In fact, it can be a lengthy process because there will be a lot of questions and the answers will not come easy.

You will probably have a hard time learning to ignore the narcissistic behavior, but you can focus on yourself. Years of emotional abuse have possibly disconnected you from your real feelings. It's high time to reconnect with the feeling of love and affection. You can look back at your childhood and think about the times that your father showed some love to you. It may have been a rare occurrence, but when it did happen, you knew that the feeling came from a place of love. It could be little things such as walking in the park or watching football. You cherished those moments because they make you feel loved despite the criticisms and the sporadic availability.

Seeing that you are loved, you can realistically look at your father for what he is. You can grow accustomed to his blocks to loving, but it should not stop you from knowing and getting the kind of love you would want from someone else. You can begin to expand your definition of love so that you are not limited to the deficient love that your father provides.

If you can separate your experiences with your father from the experiences you have as a grown-up with an identity of your own, it is possible to have a relationship with your father. It is a slow process that does not guarantee a payoff, but it is worth trying.

Reconnecting

If you have been apart for a while, reconnecting with your father entails a lot of compromising. Because you've come from a toxic relationship, chances are you don't have many common interests. You can propose activities that you think would interest both of you. It doesn't matter if it takes several suggestions and proposals, the important thing is that you agree to something that you like, even if it is not on the very top of your list. By compromising, each of you loses and gains but no one gets the upper hand. You get to be your own person and he cannot wrest control of the situation.

Having your own choice and viewpoint and giving them weight can make your father feel defeated. He would soon realize that the power of decision-making is no longer exclusive to him. Getting to a mutual decision could be a big blow to his ego because he is not used to sharing the power of decision with you. He would feel the pain of relinquishing some of his power to you.

It is important to stand firmly on your ground because your narcissistic father is still capable of manipulating you. If you don't recoil from the process, you'll realize that he is carrying a burden and not you. The weight of not having total control of you messes up his mental and emotional processing. But that is a problem that he has to solve on his own or with the help of a professional. Your only goal is to reconnect with him and find an activity that is pleasurable for both of you.

When you find a common ground, you can have a relationship that is much more balanced. Keep in mind that there are limits in how you relate with your father after a long time apart. Since he will not change his ways, all he could is adjust to the situation that you have created. Of course, he would try to make you revert to your submissive ways, but if you stand your ground, you are in a better position to fight the urge to submit to his ways.

Eliminating Interruption

Narcissists often love to interrupt because it is an effective way to kill the speaker psychologically. Interruption stops the speaker's train of thought dead on its tracks. In a conversation with your father, you could find him interrupting you several times to regain control of the moment. In his mind, he would not allow you to complete your thought because he is trying to get the momentum back to his side. It is unacceptable to him to relinquish his influence on the conversation.

When he starts his monologues, it signals his return to power. His goal is to make you listen and just fade away from the conversation. You must not let this happen. If he interrupts you, let him finish his monologue, then pick up where you left off until you finish your story or thought. It has to be a give-and-take kind of interaction, so no one gets to monopolize the conversation.

It wouldn't be fair to you if the shared activity is dominated by your father. If you let the conversation go that path, then you run the risk of surrendering to his whims. He would try to make you see that his choices and decisions are the desirable ones. The child in you will want to agree to this to win his praise, but the newly-illuminated adult that you are would recognize that this is just his ploy to get you back to your old submissive ways. The best way to handle this is to show your disinterest in his choice or decision. If you underreact, you are sending the message that you have to be involved in the decision-making as well. If what he chooses or decides on is of little interest to you, change the topic to what interests you both.

Limiting Time Together

Even if you and your father agreed to compromise, his narcissistic arrogance could continue to dominate the conversation. Reconnecting with him doesn't mean constantly being in each other's company. If you feel uncomfortable, you could change the way and the amount of spend time with him.

If his talking demolishes you, you can avoid this by setting time for non-conversational activities where there can be less talk and more enjoyment. Activities like watching a movie or a concert, visiting a museum, or watching a sporting event would be an ideal activity where conversation would be kept to a minimum. It would be an enjoyable activity and less stressful for both of you because no one is trying to out-talk the other. It is a way to establish boundaries even if your father has never respected your personhood.

Limiting your time together to enjoyable moments can lessen the frustration and disappointment that your father feels for suddenly having to deal with set boundaries. It has to be emphasized that your goal is not to seek vengeance or settle the score. Your goal is to reconnect and have a somewhat healthy relationship with your narcissistic father without experiencing abuse and cruelty.

Learning to Love

It may seem too much to ask for a positive response from a narcissistic father, let alone love and affection, but the process is meant for both of you to learn to love that you can appreciate. You are not asking for a love that your father cannot give because that is a dead end. A narcissistic father has a love for his child, no matter what, but it is not the kind of love that a child needs.

You are trying to build a kinder relationship with your self-absorbed father so that you develop compassion for him instead of anger and resentment. The process of reconnecting offers the opportunity for both of you to feel. It doesn't matter if you find out that there is so little love in his heart for you. The important thing is that the love is there. If you can accept the limitations of your father, you can allow yourself to feel the love that you actually have for him, despite what he had put you through.

When to Cut Ties with Your Father?

In an ideal world, all parents are good and nurturing to their children. However, the reality is a different scenario. Parent-child relationships can be so dysfunctional that it requires a good amount of work to fix. Society and culture dictate that family is important in the development of children. But how can a family nurture children when the father instigates the abuse and toxic relationship?

Despite the pressure to keep the family intact, it is reasonable and appropriate for you to set boundaries, including limiting contact with your father. It can be tremendously less damaging to distance yourself from your father than have him continue to wreck your self-esteem.

When the relationship becomes extremely destructive even with limited contact, you have the choice to cut ties with your father either for a while or completely. Staying in a toxic father-child relationship even when it negatively affects you emotionally, psychologically, and physically can shatter you even more, which can slow down your healing and recovery.

If you feel that the relationship is worth saving, then you can choose to initiate contact as you see fit. But if you think that it can only make you feel worse than you already do, then cutting out your dad from your life is a difficult but perhaps necessary choice. The decision is yours to make, but it is very recommendable that you choose to talk to someone beforehand, either someone close you trust or a professional.

Types of Contact

When you are mentally and emotionally strong enough to deal with your father and ready to resolve issues with him, you can decide on what type of interaction you'd like to have. The decision must be based on your readiness to face him. His level of narcissism also plays an integral role in the decision-making.

- **Civil Connection**

  This is the most common type of connection wherein you are aware that the contact will not result in an emotional bond or relationship. It's simply a polite interaction devoid of expectations. You're not expecting a sudden change in his treatment of you. It is the kind of connection wherein you have come to accept the way he is and you're okay with it as long as he doesn't cross the line. Your sense of self is solid enough that you're able to set boundaries. You are confident that no matter how he tries to suck you back into the dysfunctional relationship, you will not give in.

- **Therapeutic Resolution**

  Fathers with less narcissistic traits can be open to therapy. Your father may be willing to go through family therapy if he genuinely wants to work through your relationship issues. You can choose this route if you feel comfortable with it and he is onboard without manipulation.

Therapeutic resolution can involve your mother and siblings as well so that you all can work out your issues as a family. With a trusted therapist at the helm, your entire family may just find the healing that it needs.

- **No Contact**

  When a narcissistic father is on the extreme end of the NPD spectrum, the decision to go "no contact" could be necessary for your well-being. If your father is too toxic and continues to be abusive to you, being around him can be too damaging.

  Full-blown narcissists are considered as "untreatable" because they are not receptive to input, and they are likely to reject therapy. They have no accountability, and they have no desire to change because they don't think there is something wrong with them in the first place. This is a huge decision to make and should only be made if it is a hopeless case.

It is normal to struggle when making contact decisions because you are making a choice that will affect your future relationship with your father and the rest of your family. It is an important decision to make because you are not influenced by an authoritative figure. Your authentic self is brought to the surface and your decision is entirely your own.

If you don't feel it necessary to cut ties completely, then I recommend that you instead generally spend as little time and energy on your father as possible without turning to the drama of a "break-up". It can be energy-exhausting for you to make and live with such a huge decision which is worth keeping in mind. Cutting ties will most likely not make you feel better inside because the damage has already been done. It will just remove you from any further damage.

8

Getting Rid of Negative Introjection

The process of trying to save the relationship with your narcissistic father is long and arduous. It is not easy to understand why he put you through years of emotional abuse. What makes it even more difficult is that while you're trying to find answers to your questions, you are also trying to patch yourself up and learning to appreciate yourself for who you truly are and accept your lot in life.

Many victims of narcissistic behavior react by moving towards closure as fast as they possibly can. It is their choice because they do not have a clear understanding of what narcissistic personality disorder is. Closure will not make the negative things magically go away, but it can make you feel dead inside. What you need is to find a middle ground wherein you can learn to discriminate every negative opinion or comment hurled at you.

You have to keep in mind that you do not have to absorb all the harsh and hateful comments about you. What you need is to learn to evaluate all the negative things before you accept them as true. If you know that they are not valid, you can disregard them like rubbish. Of course, this is easier said than down because you've been raised and exposed to extremes. There was never a middle ground and it's a huge challenge to find it.

Even if you've reconnected with your slightly mellowed down version of your father, there will always be that restrictive narcissistic father residing in your head, feeding you negative words. It's like the voice of criticism that makes you feel deficient. It stops you from trusting yourself and it prevents you from taking the necessary steps to change your outlook in life.

The problem with having unwanted negative criticisms in your head is that no matter how much you hate them, you succumb to the messages and believe them to be true. You want to reject the false inputs, but you have no clue how and where to start. Your response to the negative thoughts is key to learning how to reject them.

Silencing Negative Introjection

Introjection occurs when you internalize the ideas of other people. In the context of your relationship with your father, it is his negative ideas that reside in your mind. You adopt his beliefs about you even if they are far from the truth. You identify with his distorted ideologies reflexively without evaluation or analysis.

Sigmund Freud characterized introjection as a defense mechanism usually used by children or adults to cope with emotionally unavailable parents. That judgmental voice in your head continues to reassure you that a little bit of your father is present even if he is not. If the negative introjection lingers, you will never get rid of feelings of worthlessness, incompetence, and deficiency. You'll find it difficult to find your true sense of self.

If left unchecked, the negative introjection will make you self-critical. Internal conflict may also arise because you are unable to reconcile inconsistent concepts—your longing for your father's attention and the ill-effects of his narcissism on you.

You need to understand that the measure of emotional and mental health is the state of self. If you are experiencing an overwhelming inner turmoil, then it means you are far from being in a healthy state. Silencing the negative introjection requires deliberate and purposeful thought and effort. You need to treat it as foreign to your own self. It is not supposed to be there, and it is overstaying its welcome. You need to isolate it by identifying it as a non-self. It involves changing loyalties.

When you were raised by a narcissistic father and perhaps an enabling mother, your loyalty to your father outweighs your loyalty to yourself. If you try to reverse the situation and put yourself first, you will be adjudged as selfish. This is where the inner conflict comes in. You want the circumstances to change but the conflict within you prevents you from taking your side.

Perhaps the silver lining is that negative introjection is not always at full strength. There are times when it is strong and at times, it is so weak that you can ignore it completely. It is a long-term battle with your own self, but outside intervention can make lasting changes. Therapy helps to bring back logic which weakens the introjection.

Setting yourself free from the negative introjection requires removing the childhood expectations developed early in life. The pressure that it brings makes you think that your child self is in charge of your being. But you have to understand that you are now an adult with adult needs, expectations and responsibilities. Your childish desire for your narcissistic father to meet your needs and expectations is just wishful thinking. Your adult self should remove the addicting illusory expectations from your system by getting inputs from people who are fighting a similar battle.

I have experienced tremendous value from group therapy as an adult child of a narcissistic father, who in my case was also an alcoholic. It helped me to realize deeply that I am not alone (not just as a mental idea) and to gain insight into other people's similar issues, which helped me as well. And it helped me to have an outlet for my emotions. Not so much regarding him, in fact, the group was helping me a lot more with my day-to-day problems and relationship stuff with other people. But a lot of those problems of course derived from having such a troubled upbringing regarding (both) my parents.

Group therapy can truly help you see that you are not alone in your ordeal. There are other people like you who have a negative self-image because they were raised by a narcissistic parent.

The distorted image of yourself can be cut by relating to someone who can provide you love and affection. When you are loved and nurtured, the negative introjection will loosen its grip on you.

Children of narcissistic fathers are often taught that there is only perfection and failure; there is nothing in between. This is a limited view of life because there is no more room for improvement and growth. If you can open yourself to creativity, you'll see that there is a whole spectrum of visions and infinite dreams. You'll realize that life is not just perfection or failure; there's so much in between that makes life worth living. Creativity allows you to become the person that you've always wanted to be. You'll remember the pleasures you get when you have the freedom to do things your way.

You do not have to always meet an external standard set by your father. You are so much more than your father's opinion about yourself. The problem is that the years of being under the watchful eye of your father taught you to overvalue what you receive from him and undervalue what you are capable of. You've probably lost the ability to think clearly for yourself because your ideas are always criticized and adjudged as wrong and invalid. Every reaction you get from him is a form of condemnation. The result is that you become afraid to satisfy your personal desires. You always measure yourself based on the unrealistic metrics set out for you, knowing full well that you would never meet them.

When you learn to separate yourself from those standards, you will realize that your values and happiness need not be tied to your father's measure of success such as money, fame, beauty, and power. There's more to life than trying to impress your narcissistic father whose values are flawed and distorted to serve his sense of grandeur.

Unfortunately, your life and vision are shaped by a narcissistic father who wanted you to see the world his way. His aggressive and destructive pride harms you in ways that he would never acknowledge. He doesn't realize that while he was busy fulfilling his wishes and desires, he is hurting you deeply. Although he makes you feel that you are an extension of himself, you end up having a completely different experience from him. His needs are satisfied, while your own needs are barely heeded. You always get the short of the stick. If you so much try to break his protective reverie by standing your ground, you get the brunt of a horrible reaction. He is too blinded by his self-centeredness that he fails to see your motives and desires. The critical reactions that you get from him cause additional pain.

The narcissistic falsehoods that were fed to you can cause nothing but misery because you are trained to act in ways that please only one person. It was always about him and never really about you. When you don't measure up, you expose your weakness, which only makes him stronger albeit superficially hence it strengthens the ego.

You didn't have a choice as a child

but you do now.

9

Road to Recovery

Healing and Recovery

While you learn the truth about your narcissistic father, you are also slowly establishing your sense of self. The more you discover your true self, the more you loosen your father's clutch on you. It does not mean you're over the hump; it just steers you to the path of recovery.

You may be itching to detach yourself from your father and completely disappear from his life, but this could potentially steer you in the wrong direction. Going "cold turkey" may be an enticing option, but it will not resolve the issues and will not release you from the pain. If you desire inner peace, you will not get it without recovery work. Simply taking yourself out of the equation without completing your recovery and healing will not accomplish what you have set out to do.

Before you take any action, you must first evaluate the situation and the status of your relationship with your father. As an adult, you have the freedom to separate yourself physically from your father and only make contact when circumstances require you to do so. However, that kind of set-up resolves nothing.

It is advisable to first work on your own recovery and take adequate time to allow some of the emotional wounds to heal. The decision to contact your father could be made when you have gone through the process of acceptance, grief, and separation. When you have built a stronger sense of identity you could make contact with your father. Reconnecting with him prior could undo the progress you have reached so far.

Steps to Help You Recover from Narcissistic Abuse

1. Disconnect temporarily.

The temporary separation from your narcissistic father will allow you enough space to work on yourself. You need to have this time away from the toxic relationship to sort yourself out. It keeps the focus on yourself, so you don't have to deal with judgment, negative comments, and emotional abuse.

2. Set Boundaries.

Before the healing can commence, you need to shield yourself from the one causing you so much pain. It would be difficult for you to work on yourself when you are still in the same space as your narcissistic father. Physically removing yourself from him will allow you to disengage effectively. Blocking communication will let you drown out the negative noise and allow you to hear yourself who have been silenced for so long. But more than anything else, setting boundaries is having the courage to say "no". You don't need overly critical people in your life as you build self-confidence and self-respect.

It might be very difficult for you to block communication because of the mental grip he has on you. I recommend you do it as drama-free as possible. Perhaps even make an excuse if you have to.

3. Detox

This means getting all the emotional and mental toxicity out of your system. You've spent a long time around your narcissistic father, and he has abused your empathic traits. You've always been in a situation of imbalance, and you need to bring yourself back to a place of calm and balance.

To get rid of the toxicity, you could externalize it to get some semblance of purification and clarity. One effective way is to journal. Writing down your thoughts and feelings allows you to release all the negative energies that you have kept inside you for so long.

The toxic chemicals that have been generated and accumulated from years of abuse, devaluation, and rejection will be processed and broken down until you feel that the slate has been cleared. You can also do mind-body exercises like yoga, meditation, and mindfulness.

4. Acknowledge that you've been manipulated and abused.

You have to accept the fact that your very own father is the source of your pain. You have to acknowledge that you've been tricked and manipulated in an attempt to consciously hurt you emotionally. Even your very best traits were used against you and you were powerless to confront him. It may be difficult to admit that you have allowed yourself to be used and abused for his selfish reasons, but it is important to acknowledge that to help set your mind straight.

It may also be difficult to accept that the one person who was supposed to protect you hurt you the most. This was a particularly hard pill to swallow for me.

5. Forgive yourself.

Finding out that you have let yourself be manipulated all these years can make you feel ashamed. You have to understand that you were up against a man whose mission was to destroy your sense of self so you could be tricked into doing his own bidding. It is not your fault that he is that way. Forgive yourself. If you remain critical of yourself, you are just perpetuating your father's manipulation.

6. Process your feelings.

As an adult, you have a better understanding of the situation you were put through. When you were just a small child, you didn't know that you were subjected to manipulation and emotional abuse; you just took everything in without careful thought or evaluation. You just did what you were told because your father was the authoritative figure in your life, and you believed that his decisions were good for you.

Now that you know better, you have to start processing the feelings. It is okay to feel vulnerable during the process because you are doing a post-mortem analysis of the abusive relationship. It is normal to feel shame and regret for not seeing the abuse for what it was. Processing will help you connect with your intuition and trust in yourself.

7. Do a self-inquiry

The road to recovery from narcissistic abuse is paved with plenty of emotional hurdles. Many adult children of narcissistic parents refuse to return to the scene of the crime because it only reminds them of the painful negative experiences that they had suffered growing up. In some cases, it can trigger post-traumatic stress disorder. It is a difficult situation to be in because no one really wants to relive the trauma. However, doing a self-inquiry is an exceptional opportunity for emotional growth. This is because you now have an unimpeded look at your vulnerabilities.

8. Acknowledge your greatest vulnerabilities.

Part of self-inquiry is getting a dose of reality. When you are away from the source of your misery, you get to dig deep and learn about your greatest vulnerabilities. It is never easy to discover your weaknesses and frailties, but it is part of the healing process.

You might discover that your vulnerabilities are what's attracting narcissists and manipulators. Your need for security is symptomatic of your father's inability to perform his fundamental role. He fails to instill a sense of security and protection when you were a child, so you grew up with an impaired sense of security, which makes you cling to people who are manipulative and controlling.

Relatedly, your need for adoration stems from not getting enough nurturing during childhood. You're probably realizing that your father's constant disregard of your feelings made you turn to predators who were more than happy to give you attention.

The same thing is true for your need to be acknowledged by your father. Without recognizing your needs and who you are, your father made you feel insignificant.

9. Heal the child in you.

Much of the abuse and manipulation happened during your formative years which affected your cognitive, emotional, and social development. It's what's made you who you are. Your inner child had been neglected and mistreated. As an adult, you need to restore the connection with your inner child and gave him or her the love and guidance that were not provided growing up.

Therapy could be needed to bring to the surface strong and scary emotions such as anger and rage. It is like re-parenting your wounded inner child to give it the care, support, and understanding it so desperately needs to heal.

10. Live in the present

During the recovery process, you might feel that you are being pulled back into the past. This signifies that there are still unprocessed emotions that need to be resolved. It is not wrong to feel this way because the process is never linear. You go back and forth at certain points in your life to have a deeper understanding of your life and determine why you became the person that you are.

Allow time to revisit the past but don't linger. The pull of trauma and suffering may be great when we look back, but you must use them to propel you forward and not wallow on it. If you define your purpose in life, you can work on the kinks of your past and transform from a victim to a survivor.

11. Listen to your intuition.

You've been listening to other people for so long that your ability to listen to your own voice probably has been diminished. If you learn to listen to your intuition, you'll realize that it's much more reliable than other people's opinions. Your inner intuition is your guide to a new life where you are in control. It can be tricky sometimes to realize what is intuition and what is fear or something else. There are many resources for learning it, and I recommend you dig into this. Learning to listen to your intuition can be of great benefit in all matters of life. For someone with a narcissistic parent, I will say that it is imperative to learn.

12. Rest and digest.

Being in a toxic relationship puts you in a constant state of hypervigilance. You may not be aware of this but think about the times that you tiptoed around issues just because you didn't want to trigger your father. Or the times you anticipate blame, abuse, or critical remarks from people you are in a relationship with. Your sympathetic system is overstimulated, which means you are stressed out of your mind all the time.

The fight or flight mode is making you exhausted, and it is not helping in correcting the abusive relationship. You need to switch to rest and digest mode. This can be done by activating your vagus nerve. The vagus nerve is one of the most important nerves that decrease stressors. It is the brain's way to control the parasympathetic nervous system. There are ways to stimulate the vagus nerve and some of the easiest methods are taking a cold shower, singing, gargling, deep breathing, meditating, practicing yoga, and laughing, to name just a few.

13. Practice self-care.

A traumatic relationship with your father can take its toll on your mental and emotional health. You'll find yourself emotionally exhausted. The strain can have physical manifestations and when they accumulate, your body just shuts down. If you have access to therapy, take advantage of it because you'll get the counseling that you need to help you navigate your decisions sensibly. Through counseling, you can take emotional inventory of yourself and see how you're progressing.

Aside from therapy, you can practice yoga, mindfulness meditation, and journaling to help sort out your feelings. Your emotional state is a good gauge of your well-being. If the negativity fills a large space in your mind, you need to set emotional boundaries to stop it from consuming you.

14. Create and nurture healthy relationships

Your estrangement from your father or other family members could make you feel that you're alone. It doesn't have to be that way. You are encouraged to claim a chosen family made up of friends and parental figures who can have a positive influence on your life. It is in our blueprint to connect with other people and establish and cultivate new relationships when we let go of our unhealthy and toxic relationships. You must try to surround yourself with people who can help you fix what the narcissistic abuse had broken. It could be a best friend, a mentor, a counselor, or someone who can help you get back on track with your life.

Healing Emotional and Psychological Trauma

You may have come to terms with the fact that your narcissistic father has molded you into a person with a disturbed sense of self. You may have started the process of healing by slowly building yourself up and understanding how to relate to your father now that you are an adult. However, you are still struggling with negative emotions, upsetting memories, and debilitating anxiety. Even if you know yourself better and have a strong grasp of the situation, you're still stuck in a time warp.

If you are feeling extremely overwhelmed, isolated, and helpless, you are in a state of emotional and psychological trauma. Trauma destroys your sense of security and makes you threatened that the cycle of abuse will come back to haunt you.

The symptoms of emotional and psychological trauma include confusion, poor concentration, anxiety, depression, disconnection, guilt, anger, mood swings, irritability, and fear. Trauma also has physical symptoms including but not limited to insomnia, fatigue, nightmares, body aches and pains, muscle tension, and fast heartbeat.

Emotional trauma is a normal response to distressing events, but it can become a Post-Traumatic Stress Disorder (PTSD) if you exhibit several symptoms regularly and they don't ease up. PTSD lingers because the nervous system remains in a psychological shock, which makes it unable to process the emotions properly.

A traumatic event does not need to involve death. In the case of narcissistic abuse, you are trying to cope with the loss of your sense of self and security. Just like when you lose somebody you love, you have to go through the grieving process to make sense of the traumatic experience.

When to seek professional therapy?

I have said it before, but you must remember that you are not alone. There are people like you who are struggling to cope every single day. Some victims of narcissistic abuse experience the trauma in short bursts, but others deal with symptoms that refuse to go away.

Recovery from trauma takes time, effort, and patience. Not all coping methods work for everyone. What works for one person may not necessarily work for others. Every person heals at his own pace. There are many factors at play in the healing process and there is no one-size-fits-all fix. It is possible that the right coping method can only be discovered through trial and error.

You might think that the cross you bear is too heavy that you will not survive the ordeal. Keep in mind that help is always available. Seek professional help from a trauma expert if you are experiencing the following:

- Having a hard time functioning at home or work

- Suffering from extreme anxiety or fear

- Falling into a deep depression

- Unable to form or keep meaningful relationships

- Engaging in destructive relationships

- Experiencing disturbing flashbacks and terrifying memories

- Having nightmares and inability to get a good night's sleep

- Avoiding situations that remind of the traumatic experience

- Feeling emotionally disconnected from friends and loved ones

- Turning to alcohol, drugs, and uninhibited behavior to feel better

- Thinking it would be better if you were not even alive

You might have some reservations when it comes to getting therapy because you are practically sharing your inner demons with someone outside of your family or inner circle. You might think that even with the therapist's expertise, he or she is practically a stranger. Fear of judgment might be on the top of your head as you relive the experience. You should seek help from an experienced trauma specialist with who you can have a trusting relationship. Finding the right one takes time and don't settle for the first one you consulted if you feel safe or respected.

Working through trauma can be emotionally draining and potentially traumatizing in itself, so you need a trauma specialist to help you get through all the hurt and the pain without judgment or criticism.

If you are having a tough time making a decision, ask yourself the following questions:

Was I comfortable discussing my issues with the therapist?

Did I feel like the therapist understood my problems?

Were my problems taken seriously or were they dismissed?

Was I treated with respect and compassion?

Do I believe that I could trust the therapist or counselor?

Treatment for Trauma

Healing from emotional and psychological trauma

requires processing unpleasant and negative feelings, distressing experiences, and pent-up negative energies that are stifling your growth as a person. You need to undergo treatment for trauma and narcissistic abuse so that you can learn to regulate powerful emotions and use them in a positive way. With proper guidance from trauma experts, you can learn to trust other people again.

A trauma expert may use different treatment methods to ensure that you are getting the right help and support. You will be evaluated based on the severity of the trauma and how it has affected your functioning as an individual or as part of a group. Your therapist should involve you in the decision-making because you know the problem better; you just need guidance on how to navigate through the emotional debris that accumulated from years of narcissistic trauma.

Remember that there is no one single approach that's guaranteed for everyone. The success of the treatment program depends on how well the chosen therapy addresses your problems. There should be open communication with your therapist, and this can only be done if there is trust and respect for each other.

Here are some ideas for you to explore further:

Cognitive-Behavioral Therapy (CBT)

CBT is a type of psychotherapy treatment that uses a hands-on approach to solving problems. Its goal is to change attitudes and behavior patterns to deal with emotional problems.

This approach can help you process your thoughts and evaluate your feelings about narcissistic abuse and emotional trauma. It can help to make sense of why you behave the way you do by learning about your thinking patterns.

Eye Movement Desensitization and Reprocessing (EMDR)

EMDR is a type of non-traditional psychotherapy treatment that uses eye movements and rhythmic stimulation that can unfreeze traumatic memories. It integrates elements of CBT to reduce negative feelings linked to memories of traumatic events. The focus is more on the upsetting emotions that result from the traumatic event and less on the event itself.

During the treatment session, you will be asked to remember the memory of a painful event. The therapist will guide your eye movements using a hand motion technique. The purpose of the technique is to desensitize you and allow you to process the negative feelings and recognize that you don't need to hold on to them. The negative feelings will then be replaced with positive thoughts which will be reinforced in future sessions until you no longer experience the trauma when memories of the traumatic event are brought to the surface.

Somatic Experiencing

This is a holistic approach that focuses more on the physiological responses (e.g. bodily sensations) that occur when a person experiences an overwhelming traumatic event or memory. The technique allows the body to complete the full sequence of responses to a threat or danger without interruption. When the body overcomes the threat, it discharges excess energy through shaking, trembling, crying, or other forms of physical release. This allows the mind and body to reset completely.

Restoring the nervous system to its baseline allows the normalization of the cycle between alertness and rest. During excitation, the body and mind are stimulated to react to danger. The resting state, on the other hand, allows the emotions and sensations to settle down in preparation for the next alertness cycle, which demands energy. The technique of letting the body feel all sorts of sensations allows one to identify what is pleasurable and what is distressing. It allows the proper functioning of the nervous system, so it processes emotions as they come.

Body Psychotherapy Sessions

Body Sessions is a holistic therapy treatment wherein emotional baggage and stress are released through a technique that incorporates massage, breathing exercises, and pulsating movements. It is believed to have a soothing and cleansing effect on the mind and body. This treatment relieves muscle tensions, inflammations, and swelling which promotes improved blood circulation.

The main goal is to work on the whole body to release the negative energies and let the positive energy flow unobstructed. The sessions allow the body to become more self-aware. It encourages the release of emotions by responding to touch; something that victims of trauma tend to avoid.

Rosen Method Bodywork

This method deals with the psycho-somatic symptoms and can help integrate the bodily and emotional/mental experience while identifying unconscious patterns of muscular holding, feeling, and behavior.

It is a form of body session, where the therapist's hands are gently placed on your body to release the tension build and emotions that are connected.

Through the Rosen Method, you can:

- Bring out your natural capacity for movement, for emotion, for expression

- Stop reinforcing old habits that are causing tension and discomfort

- Cultivate awareness of your body in the present moment

- Find a somatic way to practice deep listening in a relationship

- Learn to mobilize your parasympathetic nervous system

- Reveal unconscious beliefs and feelings

Group Therapy

Children of narcissistic fathers can learn from one another when they go to group therapy. By being in a group of people with the same problem, you will realize that you are not alone in the struggle. There are people like you who are having a difficult time coping with emotional and psychological trauma. You can benefit from the different coping strategies they used and the breakthroughs they've had. Group therapy is also an opportunity for you to create relationships and develop new friendships.

***

Whether the approach you take is self-help, individual therapy, or group therapy, you'd realize that the coping strategies and techniques always lead to developing your real sense of self. It is a weakness that your narcissistic father has exploited and abused over the years. You can change your weakness into strength through therapy treatment. By shedding all the biases against yourself, you are reverting to your naturally strong self with a unique identity and voice.

The road to recovery is long and filled with obstacles to hurdle. It has many stops and starts and a lot of dead-ends. Nothing is easy when everything you believed in turned out to be distorted and misrepresented. But you'll discover that if your real self emerges from all the emotional debris, and I'm confident that you will find that the journey to recovery from narcissistic abuse is worth all the hardships and struggles.

10

Final Notes...

I'd like to thank you and congratulate you for transiting my lines from start to finish.

I hope this book was able to inspire you to take the monumental step to change your life's circumstances. It takes courage to admit that you have been a victim of narcissistic abuse.

The next step is to accept that there is absolutely nothing wrong with you and practice that acceptance every single day. There is a very good reason you are struggling in life and take yourself seriously in that regard. Apply what you have learned and get the help that you need from therapists or people from your support system. Your road to recovery has already started. With determination and commitment to healing yourself, you can nurture new relationships and build a better life.

I wish you the best of luck, courage, and love!

Made in the USA
Coppell, TX
03 May 2022

77362809R00072